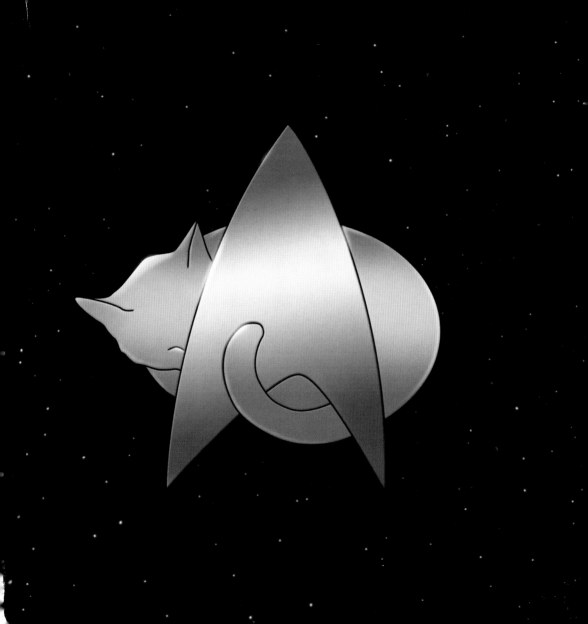

STAR TREK™
THE NEXT GENERATION
CATS

BY JENNY PARKS

CHRONICLE BOOKS

SAN FRANCISCO

LIBRARY OF CONGRESS CATALOGING-IN-PUBLICATION DATA

NAMES: PARKS, JENNY, AUTHOR.
TITLE: STAR TREK, THE NEXT GENERATION CATS / BY JENNY PARKS.
DESCRIPTION: SAN FRANCISCO : CHRONICLE BOOKS, 2018.
IDENTIFIERS: LCCN 2017044933 | ISBN 9781452167626 [HARDBACK]
SUBJECTS: LCSH: STAR TREK, THE NEXT GENERATION [TELEVISION
    PROGRAM]——MISCELLANEA. | STAR TREK, THE NEXT GENERATION [TELEVISION
    PROGRAM]——HUMOR. | CATS——HUMOR. | BISAC: HUMOR / FORM / PARODIES. |
    PETS / CATS / GENERAL.
CLASSIFICATION: LCC PN1992.77.S732 P37 2018   DDC 791.45/72——DC23
    LC RECORD AVAILABLE AT HTTPS://LCCN.LOC.GOV/2017044933

MANUFACTURED IN CHINA

DESIGNED BY MICHAEL MORRIS

10 9 8 7 6 5 4 3 2 1

CHRONICLE BOOKS LLC
680 SECOND STREET
SAN FRANCISCO, CA 94107
WWW.CHRONICLEBOOKS.COM

To Mab and Mamoko,
for reminding me how important Cuddle Breaks are.

Crew of the *U.S.S. Enterprise*
NCC-1701-D

Commander William T. Riker

Lieutenant Commander Data

Captain Jean-Luc Picard

Doctor Beverly Crusher

Lieutenant Commander
Geordi La Forge

Lieutenant Worf

Chief Miles O'Brien

Lieutenant Reginald Barclay

Counselor Deanna Troi

Ensign Wesley Crusher

Lieutenant Tasha Yar

Space . . . The final frontier. These are the voyages of the *Starship Enterprise*. Its continuing mission, to explore strange new worlds. To seek out new life and new civilizations. To boldly go where no one has gone before.

"Engage!"

"You will now answer to the charge of being a grievously savage race."

"Your alien images again shock us!"

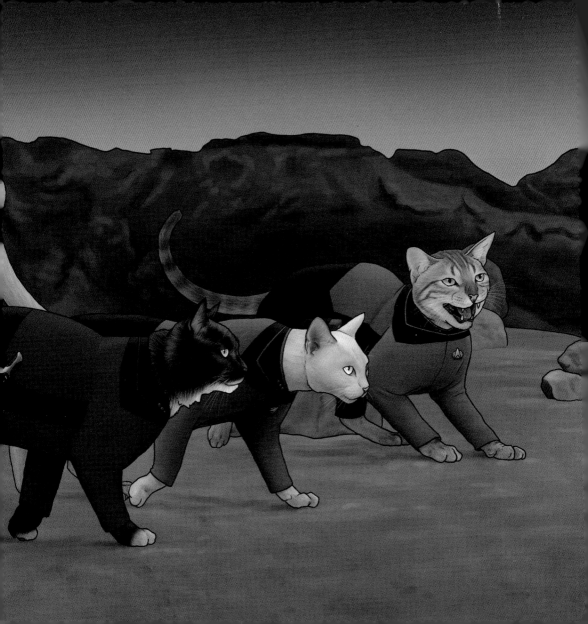

"Save your compassion; it's revolting. You offer it like a prize, when it's an insult."

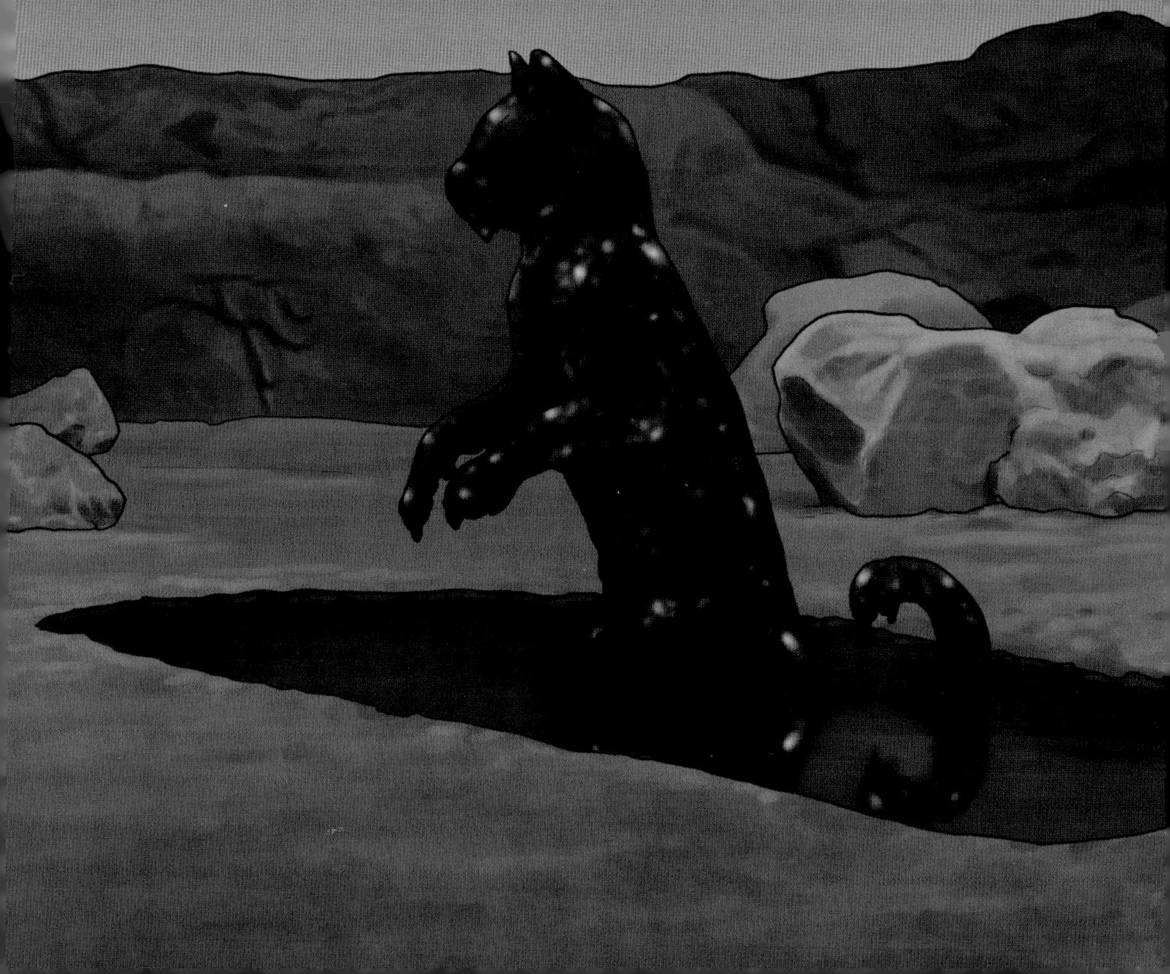

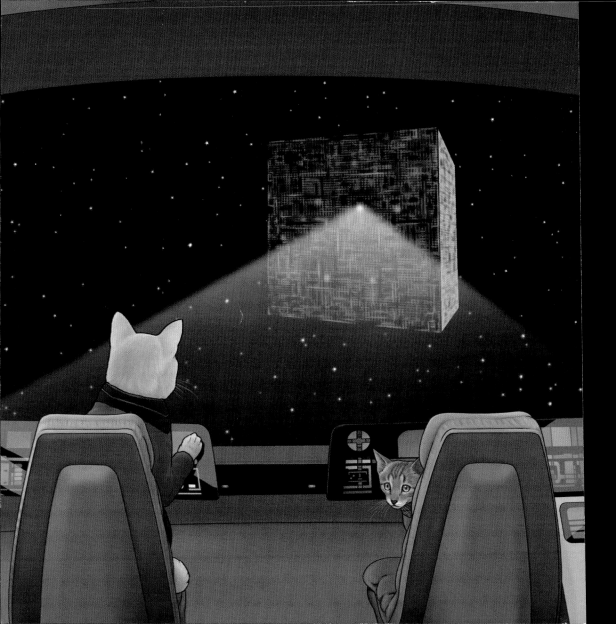

"Come Watson, the game is afoot!"

"I am Locutus . . . of Borg. Resistance . . . is futile. Your life, as it has been . . . is over. From this time forward . . . you will service . . . us."

"The next thing I know, there's a hissing ball of fur coming at my face."

"My name is Guinan. I tend bar, and I listen."

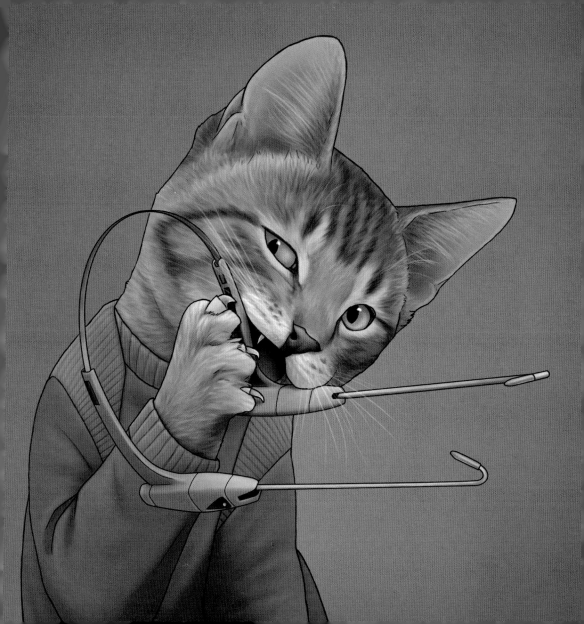

"Sir, I protest! I am not a merry cat!"

"Why're you so alarmed when I've gone to such trouble to look just like you?"

"There are **FOUR** lights!"

"Darmok and Jalad, at Tanagra."

72001 T.O.POS
020 GA.LIV
51906 GR.JEI
40776 MI.SCR

PATTERN BUFFER (QUANTUM)

TARGETING COORDINATE REFERENCE

SEQUENCE SELECT

PHASE TRANSITION COILS (PRIMARY)

15868

L00283

20

"It is a good day to die!"

"Captain, we have to eject the warp core!"

"I am Commander Sela. The woman you knew as
Tasha Yar . . . was my mother."

"My mind to your mind. Your thoughts to my thoughts."

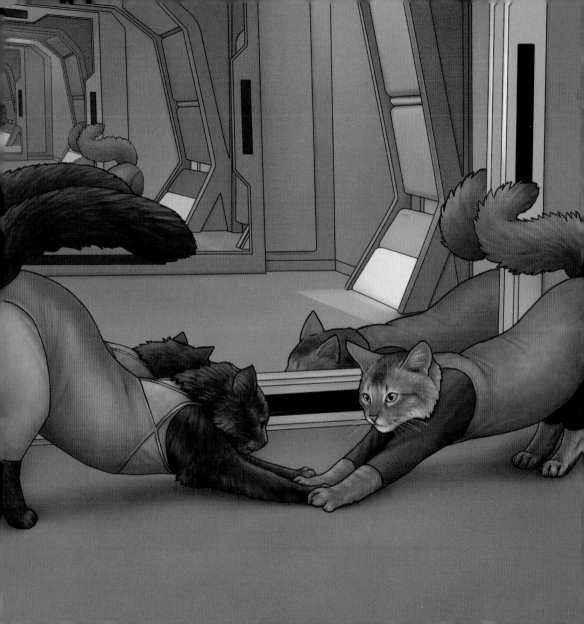

"Tea, Earl Grey, Hot."

"See you . . . out there."

EPISODE LIST: